An Imagery of Poems

ACKNOWLEDGEMENTS

The poem *Questions without Answers* originally appeared in *Mind Matters Review*.

An Imagery of Poems

By
T.M. Day

First Printing: 2014

ISBN 978-0-9863116-0-4

Bluefish Press
13769 Algranti Avenue
Sylmar, CA 91342

Ordering Information:

Special discounts are available on quantity purchases by corporations, associations, educators, and others. For details, contact the publisher at the above listed address.

U.S. trade bookstores and wholesalers: Please contact Bluefish Press Tel: (818) 261-0895; Fax: (818) 362-7929 or email bluefishpress.TD@gmail.com.

Dedication

To my family and friends, especially *Jonelle Bruno*, *Ashleigh Reese*, *Lisa M. Stewart*, and *Eileen Donovan*. Without your support, and harassment, over the years, this book would not have been possible.

A special thank you to my third grade teacher, Mrs. Corey who started me on the path to poetry at the tender age of 9.

Contents

Flickering Embers   1
One Summer's Evening   2
Arroyo   3
Inner Sanctum   4
Gift Horse   5
The Door   6
Aotearoa   7
Questions without Answers   8
You   9
A Cup Half Full   10
Chilled   11
Facing the Beast   12
Time Travelers   13
Standing on the Brink   14
Tempered Steel   15
Friends   16
Grays of Shade   17
Bodies of Water   18
Dangerous Turf   19
Snowball   20
The Martyr   21
A Prayer for Peace   22
Deep Brown Eyes   23
Circuitous   24
Dark Castles   26
Fairyland   27
Waiting   27
Extinction   28
Judean Desert Rhapsody   29

Sanctuary	30
Spotlight Diverted	31
This Place	32
Music	33
Storm Watch	34
A Native's California	35
Winged Dynamics	36
A Soul Forsaken	37
Ebb and Flow	38
Self-Fulfilling Prophecy	39
Poetry Lives	40
What Now?	41
Through the Motions	42
Afterthought	43
Art Initiates Life	44
Dreamscapes	45
The Path	46
Intertwined	47
Kingdom of Nature	48
Mind Games	49
Perceptions Askew	50
Remembrances	51
Human Interaction	52
Before	53
Awakened Horizon	54
Day In – Day Out	55
Involuntary Reflection	56
Entrapped	57
Growing Pains	58
Insipid	59
Fame	60
Just for One Day	61
Landscape	62
Two But One	63
Unscathed	64
Sliver	65

Symbiosis   66
Seaside   67
Point of Life   68
Life = X   70
Nightshade   71
Ignorance Lost   72
Let's Twist   73
Human Sacrifice   74
Passive Observer   75
Bring It On   76
Bathtub Theory   77
Dreams   78
Foiled Again   79
Instruments   80
Light and Dark   81
Eternal Discord   82
Love Poem   83
Exposed   84
Ultimate Truth   85
My Muse   86
Last Night   88
Not Again   89
Perspectives of Life   90
Primary Sense   91
Quest of the Unknown   92
Recursive Existence   93
Psychosomatic Blindness   94
Sleep – The Last Dimension   95
This One Night   96
Ode to a Sleeping Cat   97
The Old Country   98
Green Tuscan Hills   99
The Dark   100
Soul Food   101
Unforgettable   102

Flickering Embers

An instant in time
Flickers in the light of another day
Beckoning us to come;
To join the game once again

Fading embers fly
Into the air, swirling and kicking up
Over the horizon
Through the layers of cosmic soot and dust

Passing through what was
And what shall nevermore be as before
Kindling our memories
For that which we long to see again

Tugging our heart strings
With a longing and aching felt too often
Never satisfied
By either man or god

Wherein does our life;
Our immortality lie, if not in
That which survives us
And carries us into our own future

One Summer's Evening
(with a nod to Edgar Allen Poe)

Once upon a summer's evening,
As I sat there, weary, reading,
Suddenly, my senses leaving,
I rose to see the TV beaming.

Queer thought I, I don't remember,
Turning on that fiendish ember,
Perhaps it was some other member,
Wishing to my mind dismember.

So I went in my confusion,
To seek out this new illusion.
Was it just my own delusion?
Or was it some ill-thought intrusion?

Heading to the box afire,
Slowly, as if on a wire,
I felt my pulse race ever higher
As I stepped within the mire.

Then I stopped in sudden horror,
When I reached the bedroom door,
And I saw the night explorer,
'Twas the cat, and nothing more.

There the cat was, calmly sitting.
On the cable box was sitting,
While the channels, they were flitting,
And the light, it was emitting.

Still upon that summer's evening,
I continue with my reading,
Weary, though my sense not leaving,
With the TV no more beaming.

Arroyo

Houses clinging to the side of a hill
Surrounded by bushes and shrubs.
Carpets of grass, spread out at will
The lushness and color surround.

At one time a river, cut its way through,
But now there's none to be found.
The remnants of its path may lead you astray,
Through bushes and trails beyond.

Listen as the wind, blows through the trees;
In the distance – a parrot's shrill squawk.
The cooing of doves; the rustling leaves.
Lead you further inside of its realm.

Inner Sanctum

Practically strangers
A short time ago.
Now our lives entwined
Spun around each other
Not like a web, but
Rather a cozy cocoon
That keeps us safe
And warm.

What transformations
Will we encounter
Upon our metamorphosis
When we emerge
From our tender lodgings
To once again
Face life's cruelties
Without each other.

Will we be
All the stronger
For knowing each other
Or will we be
Temporarily weakened
By the comfort
We have known
In our inner sanctum.

Gift Horse

You can only give so much
Then there is nothing left.
Each time losing a little piece.
Until eventually,
You're just a shadow.

Others take and take
But not you.
You can't do that.
Your good nature's
Eroding your soul.

Always eating away
Like a slow-working acid.
Gnawing away, bit by bit.
Cutting lines in your face,
And holes in your psyche.

Sometimes it doesn't make sense.
Weighing the cost of the one,
To the cost of the many.
You can only push so far;
Watch the structure collapse.

The Door

The door's left ajar
And it won't seem to close.
At the start there's a path
And there's no one that knows
That the end's the beginning;
It's the sum of it all.
And the future's the past
But it's just down the hall.

So the questions are answered
And the meanings implied
But there's no way of telling
If we're still alive.
In the midst of the change;
At the start of the fall –
The beacon is dimming
Foretelling the pall.

There's no way of telling
In whom we should trust.
We don't know the reasons
We just know we must.
The harder we push,
The denser the wall.
Who'll be there to catch us
When we slip and then fall?

Aotearoa

Powerful spirits –
Tower
Over the picture-perfect landscape.

The primal and untouched
Oozes from every crevasse;
Spills over every cliff.

The majestic mountains
With their jagged peaks
Melt into the velvety plains.

Forests of silver fern
Slide into pale blue streams
Alive with myriad fish.

Feel it seeping
Into your skin.
Forever changed; never the same.

Reach out your hand,
And capture a dream
From an ancient time.

Questions Without Answers

Is blood really thicker than water?
Are the bonds of family fixed and unyielding?
Are the ties of mother and daughter,
Of sister and brother, intrinsic?

Where is the line of loyalty drawn?
Does respect and worship following along with
love?
We silently awake with the dawn,
Continuing on as usual.

Inside, the conflict tears at our soul.
Rational thought, gives way to irrational,
Then back again, taking its toll.
An emotional blender of sorts.

You can try to pretend that you don't care,
And maybe you don't. Even so there is the guilt.
Why don't you care; why isn't life fair?
A good question without an answer.

This is our biggest failure in life,
Thinking that all our questions will have answers.
There are no answers to explain strife.
There is no explanation for pain.

I guess that's why we have religion,
Philosophy, music, art, or the like.
Whatever it is that heals within,
And makes everything worth the trouble.

You

When you're near
I soak you in
Like a dry sponge

Your energy
Sparks the life
Within me

You are my muse
My inspiration
My soul

Your eyes are
The window
I see through

Your scent,
The bouquet
Of my garden

When you go
You leave
Only shadows

A Cup Half Full

The air is brisk; the days are short.
Bright colors all around.
The trees are losing all their leaves;
They're lying on the ground.

Like discards of, a time that's past,
There's no way to return.
If we could just bring them back,
Then no more would we yearn.

So many things past our control;
It's so hard to adjust.
Sometimes we feel so helpless,
But overcome we must.

Although it's hard, you'll make it through.
And stronger you'll become.
It makes it easier to know.
You're not the only one.

So share your problems with a friend,
And very soon you'll see,
How to survive adversity,
And once again be free.

Chilled

The chill in the air,
Cuts down to the bone.
I wonder when it again will be warm.
Wherever I am,
No matter who with,
It seems that I'm always alone.

We constantly build,
These walls 'round ourselves,
Protecting ourselves against harm.
Not realizing,
That we're keeping out
 What we love, with what we disown.

The higher the walls,
The stronger they are; impervious to all danger.
But even those soft,
Gentler emotions,
Become to us, just a stranger.

Facing the Beast

Skipping stones and fractured minds.
From within, the tale unwinds.
Jumping 'round, then back again.
Silently waits, the beast within.

With stealthy strides he makes his way
Past sullen fears and thoughts of gray.
Then to the fore, he does appear,
Although you run, he follows near.

A solemn battle, will be fought.
Your sanity is what is sought.
The beast will feed upon your will,
Resist him now or never still.

The beating in his gloomy breast,
You must forbear to pass this test.
Do not give in to his temptation,
Set your mind, no hesitation.

Iron will and nerves of steel,
Lest you be the beast's next meal.
Think your way, be oh so clear.
Approach the beast, so very near.

Step up to him, so bold and say,
"You will not take my mind today."
One more day, you've won reprieve,
Until tomorrow. . . a sigh you heave.

Time Travelers

Fleeting images,
Passing time.
Blurs of memories,
I thought were mine.

May into June,
Now into then.
Time rushes by,
Nearer the end.

The older you get,
The faster it goes.
In the blink of an eye,
Past the end of your nose.

Reach for it now,
It's already gone.
Starting with dusk;
Ending with dawn.

And so it goes
For year upon year.
One year just started,
The next one is here.

Standing on the Brink

Standing on the brink of self-discovery
I am momentarily stunned back to mediocrity
By the annoying cacophony of a stranger's phone
Summoning them to its beckon call.

The woman sitting at the table across from me
Looks as if she's never had any fun or
Called in sick because it was too nice to work.
She's surgically attached to her smart phone.

The freeway below is filled with drones
Mindlessly driving like lemmings to a cliff
Of paperwork, unending bureaucracy and
Meaningless office politics.

Suddenly, I find myself unable to move,
Paralyzed by the fear that I could be sucked
Into the vast wasteland of materialistic nirvana
Affectionately known as Corporate America.

Motionless for what seems an eternity
I finally turn in the direction of a small child
Screaming in a futile effort to be noticed
Amid the turbulent sea of urban humanity.

"Exactly," I say to myself as I quietly merge
Into the nearest wave of anonymity flowing
Against the threshold of unending storefronts
And back into the ebb of uncompromising
conformity.

Tempered Steel

Hold me in the palm of your hand
Whisper softly in my ear.
Keep me safe from the world;
Keep me next to your heart.

I'm so much more fragile
Than you would ever expect.
Like a shaken can of pop
Ready to explode at any time.

Treat me gently, as you would
Any delicate object
Made out of tempered steel.
A ticking time bomb.

Strong doesn't always mean
Impenetrable or unbreakable.
Usually the hard shell
Hides the soft pink insides.

Care for me, but don't baby me.
Love me, but don't coddle me.
Inside this concrete facade lies
A sensitive, vulnerable woman.

Friends

You left when I was young,
Before my twelfth year.
My best friend.
We laughed and cried
And played together.

On the first day of school
You were there.
We watched our moms leave.
It was OK because
We still had each other.

Hide and Seek
In the pitch of night.
Dressed all in black.
Swimming all summer
In your backyard.

Riding our bikes up and
Down the street.
Jumping curbs.
Skinned knees and
Bruised pride.

Where there was one
The other was not far behind.
Skateboards and flexies.
Daring the other to
Jump higher; go faster.

Always fighting
Like brother and sister.
Never meaning to hurt each other.
The two of us,
Both stubborn as a mule.

Grays of Shade

Sleepy clouds, snuggled next to the mountains.
The city, bathed in shades of gray.
Slo-mo scenes of the daily routine.
A breather from the usual way.

As summer turns to fall, a hush has fallen,
Over busy plans and recreations.
A chance to catch one's breath,
Before the holiday celebrations.

A time for reflecting and recollecting.
A collection of retrospection.
A nap for the nerves; line for the curves.
A break from the grind; for just a short time.

Bodies of Water

There are days
When the ebb is the flow,
And the river of life
Continues down the valley
Of consciousness.

And sometimes,
The current is dammed
By an obstacle
Of your *own* hand.

Then,
The only obvious choice
Is to reverse the flow,
And swim upstream.

Dangerous Turf

The inside of one's mind;
Is a confusing place.
Some more confusing than others.

A databank of all human experience
Stored next to the most fertile ground for
Creating anything you can imagine.

Reality and fantasy
In such close proximity
Can be a dangerous and wondrous thing.

Once the demarcation gets fuzzy
One isn't sure where reality ends
And fantasy begins.

Of course, there are some cases
Where it doesn't matter which is which
Or even whether they're different.

This is the most dangerous turf of all
Where fantasy becomes reality
And reality loses all meaning.

Then again—
Who says it ever had any
To begin with?

Snowball

They chip away
Slowly at first
Then pick up speed
Snowballing

Something snaps
What was ordinary
Now insurmountable
You're paralyzed

Frozen
Tumbling down
Mt. Everest
Picking up speed

Over and over
Circling
As a bicycle wheel
Without destination

Continuing on
Ad nauseum
Reaching the bottom
CRASH!

The Martyr

You don't listen.
Your posture, and body language;
While feigning agreement,
Show the underlying indifference.

Selfish to a fault,
Thinking you're so helpful.
Your motivation is questionable;
Your intrusiveness insufferable.

You play the martyr well
Though you don't suffer
Near as much as those around you.
We feel your pain – more than you do.

The "ultimate sacrifice" will never
Be known to you.
There's always an angle;
Underlying motives.

You administer your kindness
With a rusty needle.
Thanks, but I think I'll
Endure my own pain.

A Prayer for Peace

Blue and green mists, line the sunsets of time.
Images swirling around in my mind.
Canvases colored with the blood of the years.
Too many deaths, and too many tears.

What is it about the land that's so sacred
That animals claim and they guard every acre?
Why is it that man, refuses to budge?
For years upon years, they hold that grudge.

Forsaking all that they know to be true.
That which is righteous; it fades like the dew.
Determination, it blinds their clear sight,
Of that which is holy, of that which is right.

Their sight is so narrowed, their view is unclear.
They'll sacrifice all which they hold to be dear.
Until one upon one, they cease to exist.
One more lost spirit, devoured by the mist.

Perhaps over time, the wrongs shall be right.
Perhaps with the years, they'll cease with their
fight.
Until then we'll hope, and until then we'll pray,
That an end will be found with the dawn of the day.

Deep Brown Eyes

Your touch is deeper
Than any I've known
And it draws me
Further inside you.

As it circles and entwines,
I'm caught in its web.
A chorus of emotions surge
Through my heart as it beats.

I struggle for breath,
An effort in vain.
You've trapped me inside
The deep brown of your eyes.

Circuitous

Gnarled and twisted in knots
Was his mind
And without a thought,
He'd cleverly find
The key he needed
To unlock your past.
Patiently searching,
From first to the last.

One by one,
Through your memories he'd sift.
Through all the fun,
And each Christmas gift.
Picking away at,
That which you hold dear.
Prodding and poking
At each little fear.

He teases and taunts
At each little wound
Through all your old haunts,
To each vacant room.
And nothing you do
Can make him desist.
He's drawing you closer
And you can't resist.

Then all at once,
In his trap you're ensnared.
Done with the hunt,
He forgets that you're there.
Until you've the chance
To make your escape.
You're biding your time,
'Til you're free from this scrape.

Freedom suddenly
Seen in your view.
You've planned it so cunningly,
Know just what to do.
You wait for your move
Then pounce at your chance.
Your moves are so graceful,
They seem like a dance.

And now you're just inches
From that which you seek.
The rope slowly cinches.
You hazard a peek
At that most elusive
The end to your pain.
The more that you risk,
The less that you gain.

You finally see
That which you desire.
While gently you reach,
Tour treasure climbs higher.
And slowly the lights,
Of your eyes, growing dim.
They douse expectations,
You finally give in.

Dark Castles

Feelings don't always share
Sometimes they are quite shy.
They hide themselves away
In the creases of your mind.

Sometimes they are clever;
Use deceptive disguises.
At times they're confused,
And forget who they are.

They're very selective
About who they'll see;
Revealing themselves only
To those whom they trust.

They're a secretive group
With high membership dues;
Taking vows of silence.
They always stick together.

Their fortresses are strong
And their ramparts are tall.
You have to be crafty
To sneak into their lair.

Some never make it inside
And are doomed to wallow
In the mire of the dark moat.
Helplessly thrashing about.

Fairyland

Take me away to your ring in the forest,
And dance with me, all the night through.
I dream of your land, and I yearn for the peace
That your faith has brought unto you.

Over sidhe so sacred,
We shall pass along the way.
Carry me there to your village,
Your homeland, so far away.

Between the shadows, you'll find us.
Under the hills we shall run.
With the De Dannan forever,
We shall live in the sun.

Waiting

Like grains of sand, scattered to the wind;
Our souls intertwined, quietly wait.
One day, they shall be whole again.
Until then, we must be patient.
And wait for them to reunite.

Extinction

Sometimes, it seems, I am not myself.
"Well then, who are you?" you might ask.
It seems as though I am another like me,
But with a slightly different perspective on things.

Some might think that I have multiple
personalities,
But there is no need to fear.
For isn't it the nature of man, to recollect on things
From many different angles and views.

If we were always to think with one mind,
Shouldn't we be likened to the wolf,
Who is constantly in search of food.
Or the hyena, always engaged in mirth?

The ability to pursue many different paths,
Is what sets us apart from our fellow mammals.
And once we cease to do this,
Then we shall cease to be.

Judean Desert Rhapsody

Rippling hills blanket the desert
In sepia tones with a ribbon of green.
The sun ascends into the sky
Amid a wash of blue and gray.

Birds titter in the distance
Punctuated by a barking dog.
The radiating warmth settles on the
Rocky landscape and seeps into the ground.

On the horizon, a sleepy village
Awakens to the glory of another day,
As the fog retreats back
Into the crevasses to sleep again.

The shadows prepare to make
Their daily migration; deliberate and finite.
A gentle breeze lightly caresses
The desert grasses as they sway to and fro.

Over the centuries, little has changed
In this stark, brusque place.
On the surface it's less than inviting, yet
It's harshness beckons us in.

Sanctuary

Here I sit, all by myself,
With faint recollections of you.
Struggling with reality,
Battling demons within.

The walls are getting closer, I think.
But one moment later, retreat.
The floor, it grows cold on my feet,
And still, I dare not move them.

Images crashing through the glass,
Serve as my only reminder,
Of what lies out there, far beyond
What I know as my world.

It is here I know I must stay,
Though the outside beckons me.
I can't think of things that I miss.
I must think of that which I need.

One day, I know I will leave here,
And with it, the solace I've known.
For now I continue to live,
Safe from the fears of my past.

Spotlight Diverted

You changed me,
In ways I'm just starting to see.
Then why is it that
When I'm with you
I revert to whom
I was before.

When I'm by myself,
I'm so much more like you
Than I am when I'm with you.
Is your personality
Just too much
And I can't compete?

Do I need to have
Things on my own terms,
Cowering when I get
Too close, or do I
Just want to see you shine
In all your glory.

This Place

This place looks familiar.
I've seen it before.
The smell of the kitchen;
The socks on the floor.

At the top of the staircase,
The room to the right.
There lives a monster;
A hideous sight.

The door is shut tight,
The beast trapped within,
Lying in wait,
With a terrible grin.

He sits inside waiting,
So calm and collected.
He's timed his escape.
The moment perfected.

The room is pitch back.
No light does emit.
So still in the corner,
The giant does sit.

He's not known to many.
His torture's precise.
Carves away slowly,
Slice upon slice.

Sublime is the danger;
The damage he'll do.
And the thing is the door –
Opens only for you.

Music

Music is the soul, religion, life.
Without it, there is no reason to live.
With no music, there is no laughter, no enjoyment;
There is no salvation; no redemption.

Music is the reward for all that is unpleasant.
It's the raison d'etre, the joie de vivre.
Music makes the craziness go away;
And the stress subside.

Storm Watch

"It's just the weather," they said.
"It'll all be over in no time."

Well, that was several months ago
And here we all are
Still ruminating over some minute incident
Which occurred ages ago.

"Let's just drop the whole thing," I screamed,
But no one seemed to be listening.

Nondescript faces, talking incessantly
Without concern for anyone else.
Not a sympathetic ear in the bunch.
"Fine. Have it your own way," I said slamming the
door behind me.

"Let them have their petty discussion," I thought,
"Who needs them anyway."

Tiny droplets, dripping, dripping, dripping,
"Who do they think they are anyway?"
Dripping, dripping, dripping.
Gray upon gray upon . . .

Flash of light; thunder crack.
Chilling cold; down to the bone.

A Native's California

Waves crashing toward the shore –
  Gulls looping and diving.
    Palms dancing in the breeze.

Sidestepping crabs traverse the sand,
Attempting to avoid the many dangers.

Surfers silhouetted against an orange sunset –
  Acting out a primitive ballet of the sea.
    The ocean builds the shore, then tears it down.

Silently, the sun turns down its bed,
Sliding between its sheets of red and orange.

And so another day ends in this land –
  Of fantasy and truth; Of reality and dreams.
    Where the crazy and bizarre come to thrive.

What's the attraction to this place?
It's simple – it's all that I've ever known.

Winged Dynamics

Gracefully riding the air currents,
Master of all –
Above and below.

Unrestrained,
Like the air,
Or the ocean.

The beauty of nature,
Envelopes your being.

Touring this way,
Now what.
Swooping down with ease.

Now the prey's in your sights,
And you plunge –
To the ground.

Just as fast, you rise up
With your trophy in tow.

Beautiful *and* Deadly.

A Soul Forsaken

And so I descend into the pit.
The pain within,
Becomes more than I can bear.

Like a pup taken from its mother,
Or a Siamese twin torn from its other half,
I feel like less than what I was.

I feel an aching,
A longing,
A void which nothing can fill.

The blackness comes and goes.
It comes upon me without warning,
And consumes me.

I try to continue,
As if nothing has happened,
But it is far from easy.

Like a soul, longing for eternal grace,
I pray, although I know not to whom.
I only know of what I pray.

I pray for the emptiness to be filled;
For the void to once again,
Be inhabited by that which has left.

Ebb and Flow

Swimming . . .
Ripples in the sand
Appear at once
Then suddenly no more.

Errant cobwebs
Cover memories, long past.
Whisper –
Promises within.

As I straddle the abyss
I question my motives.
Why am I drawn
To this place?

So many moments
To seize.
Why am I stuck
In this particular instance?

Beyond the ordinary,
Lies that to which
I am destined.
Yet I hesitate.

Why does my fate
Frighten me so
That I am frozen
Where I am?

Self-Fulfilling Prophecy

Quiet silhouettes pepper the walls.
Shadows rise and fall as the tide.
Moonbeams dance with the mist.
Another day has ended.

As the day's toils are erased from our minds,
Our hearts lift to face that which lies ahead.
Ever hopeful, we are held in anticipation,
Of that which we hold dear.

Without this anticipation, we would be lost.
Forever obscured by the ordinary and the usual.
We must strive to seek the unusual.
And therefore rise above all else in the world.

Immortality lies not in making your mark for
eternity,
But in making your mark every day;
In striving for that which others shy away from;
In experiencing the most you can each day.

Until you find your essence,
You can share it with no one.
Until you find your peace,
You can give no peace.

Poetry Lives

Poetry lives . . .
In the back of a bus;
Next to the used piece of gum
Crumpled up beside yesterday's paper.

Poetry lives . . .
In the darkened streets;
Underneath the cardboard box
Functioning as today's humble shelter.

Poetry lives . . .
In a sidewalk café;
Between the double-latte soy decaf
And the dog-eared literary novel.

Poetry lives . . .
On the playground;
Climbing the monkey bars –
Escaping down a spiraling slide.

Poetry lives . . .
Inside the wretched;
Abandoned by life and society
Continuing to possess great hope.

Poetry lives . . .
In a third-world country;
War torn, striving to gain
Freedoms they have never known.

Poetry lives . . .
In the smallest crevice;
Where you would least expect it
Deep inside of us all.

What Now?

Riveting images plastered against the past.
Dominant overtones interrupting the calm.
Waves of emptiness, crested by anxiety and stress.

Unknown desires, wants, needs -
Displaying your psyche for all to see
Vulnerability, loss of control.

The pit in your stomach,
Blacker than the black hole of Calcutta.
Restless dreams, childhood fears.

Out-of-control, over the edge.
Hauntingly plagued.
Shut out the world and live.

Through the Motions

Images passing
Behind my eyes.
Sorrowful dreams,
Forgotten lies.

Triumphs foregone
Never come back.
Tragedy played
Over en masse.

Deep in your soul
Things never heard.
Singing through now,
Like the songs of a bird.

Over and under
The truth never lies.
Caught in the wishes;
Trapped in the sighs.

Repeat through the day
Until there's no more.
Tired of the traffic,
Like a ten dollar whore.

Lay down forever
Numb to the pain.
Nothing much ventured;
Nothing much gained.

Afterthought

Lofty dreams and high ideals
While all around you
Reality squeals

Shut yourself in; toss out the key
Safe in your skin
As you drown in the sea

Stuck in the mire; out of your mind
Your ultimate fate
Is slowly resigned

The trial is over, before it's begun
Dejected and hurting
The contest is done

The root of the problem, it comes to bear,
Don't take the trip
If you can't pay the fare

Art Initiates Life

Life without art is cold
Stiff, like wet socks left out in the snow

It makes your soul empty
Vacuous and black – lacking substance

At first, you don't notice
The change is gradual, bit by bit, sucked away

Then one day, it happens
You can't breathe. The simplest task is a chore.

The burdenous weight is too much
Your essence collapses under the pall

Life without art is stuffy
It gets monotonous too quickly, dragging on

Without self-expression
The world is a prison, stifling at best and
suffocating at worse

Creativity is what separates us
From all other forms of life.

Without it, we are robots
Aimlessly going on about our daily tasks

Day in and day out
Trudging along on a never ending road

Soulless and lifeless
Without end and without substance

Dreamscapes

Reality itself is so absurd,
I wonder why anyone bothers
With fantasy.

Unless,
Of course,
It's merely a counter-balance.

I've always been an advocate of dreams.
Day dreams, pipe dreams,
Sweet dreams, night dreams.

Our unconscious,
After all,
Has a much easier time coping.

The Path

Old habits are hard to break
You always find your way back
No matter how far you've come
The path is too clearly defined

You think you've moved on;
It's overgrown with scars and pain
But once you start,
There is no turning back

The old wounds, now fresh,
Hurt all the more, since you
See it all ahead of time
Like slow-motion in your mind

It's no one's fault but your own
You have the power to make it stop
But the pain is so familiar and sweet
It rushes through your veins like blood

And the hole that was filled
Is now empty once again
The search for a plug has begun
Back through the path, to its source

Intertwined

Intertwined,
Around and back,
Over and through,
Take up the slack.

When you're cut
I will bleed.
When I'm hungry
You will feed.

Experiences shared,
As ever, sublime.
I am your melody,
You are my rhyme.

Hard to create,
A mix so divine.
A pairing so delicate;
A friendship so fine.

Bonds that were forged,
By Hephaestus on high,
Will never be severed,
Though people may try.

Friendship so dear,
Refined to an art.
You always will be,
Close to my heart.

Kingdom of Nature

Blades of grass, reaching toward the sky,
Sway in the gentle breeze.
Little birds, singing and playing, flit
Between the shade trees.
A beam of light, strong and unbending,
Penetrates the brush.
Several squirrels, running and chattering,
Travel in a rush.

Overhead, a lonely hawk,
Circles 'round and 'round,
With an ever watchful eye
Turned downwards toward the ground.
Below, within the underbrush,
Slides a hungry snake;
Stalks the naïve prairie mouse
Near the placid lake.

As the day begins to turn
Slowly into night.
All the creatures stop and rest,
Weary of their plight.
Tomorrow is another day,
To hunt and run and play.
For now, they sleep and dream about
Adventures of the day.

Mind Games

The mind is so good at playing its tricks.
That you seldom know they are played.
Back in the corner all hunched and bent over,
It's plotting and chipping away.

And it's one piece right here, another from there.
The raveling so slowly begins.
Together, quite well, the quilt work takes hold,
Creating a cohesive blend.

And then all at once the bond starts to fail.
Shards, and then bits soon detach.
They fall by the roadside,
Leaving the rest, to endure countless perils
unmapped.

Dismantled, the whole no longer exists.
Scattered throughout the scene.
Fractured and incomplete as you struggle,
To make yourself whole again.

Perceptions Askew

Houses dot the landscape and surrounding hills.
From above, they appear as insignificant
As a fly spec upon the window sill.

Curious how things appear differently,
Depending on your point of view.
How can one's perception be so easily altered?

It must be wonderful to see the world
With wide-open spaces.
Watching the horses and cattle
Grazing across the plains.

To see it all, when it was new and untouched.
Now that would have been a glorious thing.

Remembrances

Swirling images,
As discarded leaves,
Filter through our selective consciousness.

Some will fly away,
While others will stay,
Etching themselves onto our brain cells.

The ones that will stay,
And those that will go,
Are as random as the toss of a coin.

Or so that is what you think.
There is some logic,
Deep buried in your psyche.

Some thought long gone,
May return at a later time,
Triggered by some uncertain connection.

Human Interaction

Pinks and purples of days gone by,
Sink in the cracks of my mind.
Reminding me of those thing I miss;
And I'm hoping again soon to find.

Those who we've touched, and been touched by,
Become what we know as ourselves.
Memories and friendships, one by one,
Are added like books to the shelves.

Just as events can shape our lives,
So do the people we meet.
The briefest encounter can be –
Like softly played music, so sweet.

So open your heart and open your mind,
To all who would share time with you.
What they can give, cannot be bought,
But it can be kept and shared too.

Before

At some other time,
In some other place.
The curves of your body;
The lines on your face –

Tell me I knew you,
I knew you before.
Perhaps even closer;
To my very core.

From that exact moment
The two of us met.
There was something about you,
That time won't forget.

Then I knew that our lives,
Once before had been crossed.
Souls meant to be one,
Through death, never lost.

Awakened Horizon

Tiny waves caressed the jagged shore,
While zephyrs nudged the bending trees.
The aging timbers of the old ship,
Creaked and groaned with the tide.

The sea-weary travelers strained their necks,
To glimpse a view of their new home.
Like others who had come before them,
They had left the known to venture into the
unknown.

The land their eyes fell upon,
Was not unlike that which they had left.
The rolling hills and flowering meadows,
Beckoned them like an old friend.

What they left behind,
Seemed worlds away now,
As the waves reached out,
And pulled them closer to their new home.

The innocence of it all enveloped them,
And their minds reeled with possibilities.
Possibilities never open to them before.
Even the familiar sea gulls, were seen to them
anew.

Freedoms previously imagined were now visible,
As foes previously fought would be vanquished.

With anticipation, they clamored toward their
future,
Leaving their pasts to fade into the mist.

Day In – Day Out

Tick, tick, ticking.
Can't they stop... the... ticking.

Why can't... they... stop? Won't they?
They must stop it!

Day in – Day out.
FOREVER

Never does it cease.
Endlessly, on and on.

Droning, like a bagpipe
Far in the distance.

Incessantly going on and on.
Day in – Day out.

FOREVER

Involuntary Reflection

Glistening rivulets of rain,
Glide slowly down my window pane.
As the fire radiates,
It warms the room and fascinates.

What is in the past we see,
That we cannot just let it be.
Do we see the things we fear?
Or those we love, no longer near.

Contemplate now the season,
Which comes about without reason,
Generates some energy,
To coax us into revelry.

This façade, I can't deny,
Disturbs me much, with heavy sigh.
Wishing that the game would end,
Withdraw into the walls again.

Later, perhaps, venture out.
Assessing what has come about.
Finding that the game is done,
We wait to play another one.

Entrapped

With one fluid motion
She reached in his chest
And yanked out his heart.

He barely felt a thing.
It wasn't until much later
He realized what happened.

How could he have
Been caught off guard;
Totally unaware.

OK, maybe he wasn't
Completely unaware.
Secretly, he wanted it.

Wanted her, actually,
Since the first day
He saw her there.

He dreamed about
Caressing her bare,
White shoulders.

Kissing her deep
Red lips; holding
Her and never letting go.

Only after speaking
To her did he realize
He was entrapped.

Growing Pains

He is of my flesh.
When he's cut
I will bleed.
If he's hurt
I will cry.

Each of life's lessons
Comes in its time
And it surely is
A bitter pill
I swallow with him.

I can only shield
Him from so much
And the rest he'll
Have to learn on his own
While I watch.

Give him the strength
And give me the strength
To help him through
These difficult years
Of growing pains.

Insipid

Quietly slip in
Through an open window.
Down the hall,
Past each door.
Up the stairs
    One
        By
            One.

Creeping slowly
Barely breathing.
Slide into your room
Next to your bed.
Lifting the covers
Ever so slightly.

Ease my body
Right next to yours.
Wrapping around
Each limb
Enfolding you

Inside me.

Fame

I sometimes think fame is reserved
For those with evil in their hearts.
Lie, cheat, steal, or kill,
And you're that much closer.

Save a life, and –
Maybe you'll make the local news.
Take a life, and –
You're on the front page of every newspaper.

It seems as if society rewards
Terrible, heinous acts
More generously than
Acts of kindness and love.

Those that deserve fame
Rarely receive it.
Those that don't,
Receive it, in abundance.

Just for One Day

Tell me I'm beautiful
And make me believe it
Tell me you love me
And make me care

Make love to me
Like you're not just horny
Make me love you
Like it's not convenient

Act like we're strangers
Like we're in some movie
Two people who meet
With everything in common

Love my favorite songs
My favorite movies
Laugh when I laugh
Cry when I cry

Make me believe
You'd move the heavens
And the earth only because
I asked you to

Landscape

Reach out your hand
To capture a whisper
Lay on the grass and fly to the moon

All your desires are there for the taking
Unleash your mind
And the journey begins

Over the clouds and under suspicion
Invert your thinking
To see where you've been

Life microscopic
Is no way of living
The endless minutia, will drive you insane

Broader horizons will
Keep you more steady
The richer the landscape; the keener the wit

Vary your path and take on new meaning
Capture a glimpse of
The past yet untold

Two But One

I could easily snuggle beside you.
Just lie against your skin,
Feeling your pulsing heart;
Touching your heaving chest.

Resting my head in your arms,
As we lay here in silence.
No words are needed,
We touch each other's soul.

Never closer, we two,
Than we are now.
Hearts beating in unison,
Breathing in sync.

If you stopped breathing
At this moment;
So should I;
Not knowing what else to do.

Unscathed

Words, taken to a page
Can be a sorry excuse
For telling you what
I'm really feeling
But the ink, flows
Through the pen
Directly from my veins.

I see in you,
So much of me
And yet we are
So very different.
How can we see
The very same things
Yet feel nothing the same?

So easily,
I could have been you.
How is it then
Fate decides
What befalls whom
And who emerges
Unscathed?

Sliver

The thump, thump, thump of daily existence
Wears on you like an ill-fitting shoe
Slowly eroding, layer by layer
Your sanity; Your very being.

At some point, you're no more than a shell
A carbon-copy cutout of the person you once were
You hardly notice it's happening.
Moving slowly, like geologic time.

Each day, you lose a little piece of yourself
Family, friends, acquaintances,
Walk off with a small portion
One sliver at a time.

Shaving off pieces, bit by bit
Systematically removing that which
Makes you who you are, until you have
Nothing left that you call your own.

You are now a creation of those
Who surround you.
Struggling to keep that part of yourself
Which is sacred and truly yours.

The more you struggle, the more you sink,
Down into the abyss, until
There is no way to rise up to the top.
You have sunk into the depths of your own psyche.

Symbiosis

Shadows erupting
On the horizon
Drift and fade into the dawn

The cat silently
Stalks its prey

With cunning deftness
It lies in wait

It does what it must
And only that;
To survive

It never kills
What it will not eat

It does not gorge itself
But eats only until satisfied

It is an integral part
Of the whole
To which we all belong

A small piece
Of the larger puzzle

We are all made from the same mold
Human and beast

And it is increasingly difficult
To tell which, is which

Seaside

Here I sit beside myself,
And look across the sea.
Searching for the time I've lost,
While trying to be me.

Breathing in the salty air,
To soothe and calm my soul.
Listening to the crashing waves,
To mend the fractured whole.

Now and then, I recollect
Upon those things gone by.
Reaching for what is not there,
And asking myself, "Why?"

Bearing wounds that will not heal,
I look for what is pure.
What the future holds for me,
No one can be sure.

Aching, longing, deep within
That never will subside.
Looking for the recipe,
For happiness inside.

Point of Life?

To make more money
Than anyone could spend?
To empty your soul
'Til you've reached the end?

To learn about everything
'Til there's nothing left?
To show off your talents;
To prove you're the best?

To own a big house
On the top of a hill?
To numb all your senses
By taking some pill?

To reach out to God
And feel His compassion?
To be like the crowd
And dress like the fashion?

To slaughter your foes
While you claim divine right?
To distance yourself
From the sufferers' plight?

To follow the path
Of America's dream?
While your 2.3 kids;
Come apart at the seams.

All the while searching
For something with meaning.
But everything straight,
Seems somehow to be leaning!

Upon careful scrutiny
The flaws, all too clear.
Was there ever a purpose
To our being here?

Should I just stop looking?
Why won't it be found?
The paradox put here
Will forever confound.

The point of our being
Is to find out just why.
And the Why, to discover,
The point of our lie.

And each time we fall to
The 'chicken and egg.'
Deducing it's ourselves
Who have now laid the egg.

Life = X

Life.
An endless series
Of unrelated situations
Brought together by fate and time.

Disappointment, elation,
Tragedy, fulfillment.
Pacing one against the other is the trick of it.

Getting the good
To balance with the bad.
And what of sanity? Or reality?

Does sanity not lie
In the mind of
The beholder?

When does the chore
Of everyday life
Cross the line?

When does the simplest task,
That of being,
Become the hardest of all?

And where do
All of us fit
Into this equation?

Nightshade

Mind, thought,
Body, Soul.
The borders of countries
Should be so vague.

One bleeds into the other,
As the colors of a rainbow –
Dancing across a cloudy sky.
Beauty and danger intertwined.

As the deadly nightshade
Waits for its victim,
So shall I,
Await what I seek.

Patiently, quietly,
Secretly, waiting.

Ignorance Lost

Watery dreams cascade down, into a sea of
misspent youth.
Time dwindles much like expended tissues,
Aching for a meaningless moment.
I strain to ignore the writing on the wall.

Snatches and clips of an uninspired past
Whirl and float above my head
Teasing me with reminiscences,
Glimmers of lost innocence.

Time was our servant
Bending to each whim we desired.
Now it is our master and
We have no options left to us.

If we knew what we had
Would we have let it go so easily?
Or is that the magic
Of having it to begin with?

Ignorance isn't bliss.
It's the manifestation of having
Something that you
Would never have had otherwise.

Let's Twist

Twisted and complex
The lives which we lead.
At the core of our being
The need for simplicity.

Our continuing struggle –
To piece back together
The puzzle at large,
Which is unknown.

To somehow end up
With a logical path from
The point of inception
To the point where we're at.

So the perpetual conflict begins.
Tightening the web
Which we weave
Around ourselves.

Human Sacrifice

You thought the path was clear;
The way ahead was true.
Then something happened and
Everything suddenly changed.

Now you need to sit back and
Take stock of the situation.
The path you follow from this point
Must be different from what came before.

The hazards may be the same
Or they may be different.
But they will be handled
In a much different manner.

You are changed,
Whether or not you realize it.
Your path has been altered
And you must persevere.

Before it was just you
And now there are others.
You must look out for them
And consider their needs.

And still, you must not
Forget yourself.
You have needs and desires
Which must be tended to.

You can only sacrifice
Yourself to a point.
Then you must pull back
To let yourself heal.

Passive Observer

Stranger than fiction. Stranger than you are.
Search through your mind. Search near and far.
Waiting for the answers. Waiting for a sign.
Walking straight ahead. Walking a fine line.

Skirting past the issue. Skirting through your life.
Failing to acknowledge. Failing to survive.
Ignore all the symptoms. Ignore all the signs.
Pray for forgiveness. Pray for sunshine.

Give in to your fears. Give in to desire.
Sing your own dong. Sing with the choir.
Only so long, can you flip side to side.
Only so long, can you bury your head and hide.

Bring It On

You bring it on yourself now.
You know that much is true.
Every time you suffer
The cause is always you.

You need to take a step back
And look into your past.
The pictures are revealing
From the first until the last.

You have the means to fix it.
If you change your ways.
Don't you be so hard now.
Just take it day by day.

You know that no one's perfect,
So why expect so much.
You're getting quite obsessed now
You're getting out of touch.

Kick back and let it slide some
And let the pressure ease.
You need to have some fun now
And do just what you please.

Life is way too short, to spend
Inside a padded cell.
When will you stop making,
Your life a living hell.

Stop your second guessing;
Give it your best shot.
Don't make it all into
Something that it's not.

Bathtub Theory

Contemplating life in the bathtub.

Archimedes solved his problem
While sitting the bathtub – Eureka!

Newton discovered gravity,
While resting beneath a tree.

Great discoveries are found
When you're not looking for them.

Love is found,
While lost on a country road,
Heading toward
Nowhere in particular.

Dreams

Dreams are something you wish for,
Then you tuck them neatly
Into a corner of your mind.

Silently they sleep,
Waiting for the day they will awaken
And fill your being with joy.

Sometimes they sleep forever,
Never to open their eyes to
The ecstasy within.

Sometimes they awaken when you least expect it
And are the least prepared
To deal with their onslaught.

And sometimes, if you are very fortunate,
They awaken at
Just the right time.

Foiled Again

Caught with your guard down.
Like a knife,
Reality is thrust
Into your being
Without warning,
Without provocation.

So innocently
You go about your way.
Never thinking to look
Over your shoulder.
Step, by step, by step.
Plodding along.

Suddenly
Everything you ever wanted
Is out of your grasp.
And you're sliding down
Into the abyss.

Swallowed whole
By the ineptness
Of your own naïveté.
Taken in
By the cleverness
Of your optimism.

Betrayed
By the safety
Of your ignorance.

Instruments

These instruments of torture.
How meek they appear.
Yet so delicate their pain,
That we hardly know what they inflict.

The effects are slow to surface,
But the scars are etched on your face.
The color, taken from your hair;
The laughter, emptied from your heart.

Slowly,
They eat away at your soul.
Blacken your heart,
And leave a bitter taste
In your mouth.

Light and Dark

You, with your strong color
Coming to fade me
Into the shadows
Of your life

How dare you look at me
With the disdain
Usually reserved for
A pair of unmatched socks

Jumping into the spotlight
I'm dangerously close
To all that which
You hold dear

Teetering on the edge
Of light and dark
I struggle to own
What you possess

With the unwavering confidence
Of someone, who
Doesn't realize that there
Is something to lose.

Eternal Discord

Images cascading over hopes and fears.
Backward glances at distant years.
"Never forget the mistakes of the past."
Echoes again and again 'til the last.
But natural progression, seems to avail,
And attempts to prevent it, all seem to fail.

So the sins of tomorrow join the sins of today,
Forcing you back to your worst yesterday.
And it gets so confusing, we don't really know,
The lessons we learned, and those still to go.
Like Manifest Destiny, onward we trod,
Towards the mouth of the lion, with golden façade.

Intelligence we have, but never do use.
We act like the sludge of primordial ooze.
Placating the whims of simplistic urges,
We dismiss all the blame for whatever emerges.
So what of this brain that makes us so grand,
That we rape and we pillage and torture the land.

And what of our brethren, who are sharing this
Earth,
With malice and hatred, we curse them, their birth.
The rest of God's Creatures we give little thought.
For their health and well-being, we think scarcely
or naught.
Then for all of these things we continually do,
We expect all the glory and nothing do rue.

I expect in the end, we will get our reward,
For being the essence of eternal discord.

Love Poem

For some, it's ever love they seek.
Some well know from whence I speak.
While others wait for love to come,
Love comes easier for some.

Now with your day within your grasp,
Pure happiness has come at last.
Your days of seeking now retire,
The flames of love have stoked your fire.

From now, forever, that fire will burn,
And year by year, your love will learn,
The deepness of your full devotion,
Is large enough to fill an ocean.

Exposed

A nearly extinct
Side of your psyche.
A virtual hermit
Of your internal makeup.
The fragile and vulnerable side,
Makes itself briefly known.

And for a moment,
I'm caught totally off guard.
Such a rare occurrence,
I sometimes forget that you are,
After all, only human.
To me, you are superhuman.

And why not.
Juggling tasks and priorities
With finesse and grace
Is not for mere mortals.
Most people find it hard
Just taking care of themselves.

Poetry in motion –
Tending to the care and
Well-being of others
Is not an easy task.
Those thinking otherwise,
Should be shot on sight.

Ultimate Truth

As I sit on the edge of the shore,
Watching the waves crash against the rocks,
I am reminded of what we all realize is true,
That truth itself is an incongruity,
Shaped by people for their own devices and uses.
When will we realize it is ultimate truth
Which we all seek and never find.

The ability to find the ultimate truth
Is within our grasp at birth,
But as we get older that ability fades
Too quickly, too easily, from our reach.
Replaced by this search is another,
Almost as fleeting and elusive as truth,
But not near as noble or worthy of our attentions.

It is this search which causes us to abandon
Those in need, those who are sick, those who are
weak.
Often, when the goal is reached, a greater quest,
Of more of the same, becomes the next obstacle.
We disregard our better judgment,
And fail to hear the cries and screams, of Humanity
As it struggles to survive the demands of our
culture.

My Muse

When I'm with you
It seems as though
I am not myself.
But I know this
Is not true.
In fact, I am more myself
Than at any other time.

I'm relaxed, confident,
And without a care
In the world.
I believe I can do anything,
Be anything,
Have anything,
Feel anything.

The doubt is gone,
The second guessing,
The insecurities.
Why is it that I cannot
Carry this with me
When I leave your side;
When I'm not with you?

I think perhaps,
It is that you truly
Know my heart.
In some ways, I feel
As if you know me

Better than I think that
I know myself.

Or else you see the
Promise of what
Could be me.
You see the talent
And the passion
Which I hesitate
To act upon.

You are my muse.
Of that
There is no doubt.
Your faith in me,
Is inspiration enough
To write a
Thousand sonnets.

But what good is it
If there be but
A handful of people
Ever to see them?
They must be shared
Or the inspiration
Shall be wasted.

Last Night

Last night I dreamt I was fishing,
Beside a calm lake of bright blue.
Last night I sat near the water,
Relaxed and with nothing to do.

Last night I dreamt I was falling,
Beyond the constraints of this world.
Last night I jumped to my death,
Down to my doom, I was hurled.

Last night I went to your house dear,
Behind the block wall to your sill.
Last night I found out your secret,
Tonight I will sleep with a chill.

Not Again

You're afraid it's happening again.

Last time, it was almost more
Than you could bear.
And when it was over,
You thought that was it.

Hoped that was it.

Inside, you knew that it would
Never really be over.
It would always be there—
Lingering.

Waiting for its chance.

It wasn't so long ago
That you don't remember
How your life was altered,
Some good; some bad.

Some scars will never heal.

Last time, you needed help.
This time, can you do it alone?
Did you learn enough last time
Or is the learning ongoing?

Are you strong enough this time?

Perspectives on Life

As the darkness lifted to reveal the light,
And the stillness had returned.
They stood in awe before the sight,
Of the city which had burned.

Among all the rubble and debris they found,
Were some cartoons and some toys.
And so they laughed; joked around,
Remembering old joys.

They understood well, the work still ahead,
Through efforts so much in vain.
For the moment, their fears were shed,
In actions most inane.

Primary Sense

So I wouldn't stop traffic
Is that a bad thing?
Men never notice me – *ever*.
Kids and animals love me.

They just don't know
My quirky sense of humor.
My love of art;
My sensitivity.

You just can't look
At someone and know
That they would stop to
Take a lost dog back home.

Appearances don't reveal
That someone does
Everything from the heart
With feeling and passion.

A mediocre façade
Can easily hide a soul
Craving world peace
And human equality.

Often it is the case
That the plainest
Of packages bears
The greatest gifts.

Quest of the Unknown

Slowly, the veil of the mists lifted,
To reveal that which had been eagerly anticipated.
But, when they looked on what appeared before them,
It was not awe which filled their beings.

It was emptiness.

An emptiness which was complete and all-consuming,
For that which had been revealed to them was not their salvation,
But the presentation of ultimate ruin.

Returning to their places of origin,
They vowed never to speak of the place again,
Lest the emptiness would return and consume them.

Recursive Existence

Does life have a purpose?
I often wonder.
I think that the great irony of life
Is that there is no purpose
Other than the amusement of God.
Sitting back on His heavenly throne
Watching us all
Aimlessly searching for some meaning
To the chaos called life.

Why must we find that greater purpose,
That glue which binds us all together?
Why is it that we cannot just accept
The fact that there is no purpose?
Perhaps this is what keeps us alive,
The struggle.
Maybe that is what death is,
When we finally decide that we don't care
What the meaning of life is?

I suppose then, the meaning of life is
That life has some meaning.
And it is up to the individual
To discover exactly what that meaning is.
Be it a passion for art, a career,
A family.
For everyone it is different,
But it must exist
In order for us to survive life at all.

Psychosomatic Blindness

Across the desolate plain there was nothing to be
seen.
Nothing to break the monotony of the continuous
horizon.
The flatness was reminiscent of a huge slab of
concrete.
The utter solitude was enough to make a monk
weep.

For days, on and on it continued without end.
The hunger and thirst were barely noticeable,
Compared to the emptiness within his soul.
At the very brink of insanity, he noticed it.

A small, delicate shoot of some unknown plant
Had broken through the surface of the unending
desert.
He must have watched that tiny plant for days,
weeks.
It offered little in return, other than an occasional
growth spurt.

Eventually, he could hold on to life and sanity no
more.
There he died, inches away from the little plant.
Had he continued on with his journey, he would
have found,
Over the next horizon, an end to his hunger, his
thirst, his travel.

Sleep – The Last Dimension

The pounding continues
Sometimes it's hard to tell
If it's coming from the inside or the outside.

Familiar places that never existed.
Good friends I've never met.
Animals coming to life.

Soaring high above everything.
I can see things I've never seen before.
Go places I've never been.

I've been shot,
Stabbed,
Killed.

I've fallen off cliffs;
Slept with movie stars.
Been a hero and a martyr.

I've foreseen the future;
Defied the odds;
Tested the limits.

Lying down to sleep,
I wonder what I'll dream of tonight.

This One Night

Gave you my heart,
I gave you my soul.
When you're not around,
I feel less than whole.

Through painful nights
And tremulous days –
You've been there for me
In so many ways.

Now you tell me,
You've made a mistake.
Our vows were a joke;
Commitment a fake.

I thought I knew you,
I guess I was blind.
I don't understand,
What lives in your mind.

Through all these years,
Together as one,
Now you've severed that,
To go have your fun.

You've made me think,
There's nothing to trust.
But I can't give up,
Continue, I must.

I will go on,
Continue the fight.
If I can get through,
This one night.

Ode To A Sleeping Cat

Sleeping Meedie on his back,
Legs all splayed, and tail relaxed.
Nose so pink and fur so white,
Eyes are closed so very tight.

Hush yourself, now don't disturb,
The quiet one; do not perturb.
Perfectly, he lies asleep,
Dreaming of his castle's keep.

The Old Country

When I stepped off the plane, I stepped back in
time.
A time that was older, a land that was weathered.
I walked down the streets and I heard the bells
chime,
The ringing was colder, the ringing was tethered.

The streets were uneven, the buildings were worn.
My heart filled with wonder, its beating was
quickened,
Excited by all that my sight now had borne,
The skies I walked under; its clouds as they
thickened.

I felt overwhelmed by the feelings I found.
A land I knew not; but a sense that I did.
The history and lore did I find to abound.
And the knowledge I sought, I was taken amid.

For this was the land which my blood, it was
drawn,
From the grass on the bogs and the fog in the air.
So I stared at the sun, until it had gone,
And my spirit did soar with my soul without care.

And when I returned, a piece I did bring,
Of my ancestor's land and the spirit within.
Once in a while, when the yuletide bells ring,
With my heart in my hand, I live it again.

Green Tuscan Hills

The green Tuscan hills roll
With the breath of the wind
And the branches sway
To the rhythms of the Earth

Terracotta houses
Dot the landscape
In the valley below
This solitary retreat

Amid the groves of olives
The cicada tell of their adventures;
The sun slowly closing its eyes
Ending another day

Wispy clouds blanket the sky
In a cocoon of tranquility and peace
Darker clouds on the horizon,
Foretell of storms to come

A church bell peals on the hill
Six o'clock and the evening
Is already upon us
New journeys await us tomorrow

The Dark

Light dances off the ceiling
And off the walls.
Echoes of voices
Shriek down the hall.

Tricks play on your mind.
The silence entwines
And slowly all rational
Thought will decline.

Reflections of memories
Bounce off the mirrors.
Ideals and dreams
Bounce off your fears.

Late in the night
When you should be in bed.
It's funny the things
That appear in your head.

Things that you know
Can't possibly be
Emerge before you
In all that you see.

There in the darkness,
All things are real.
Your peace of mind
Is ready to steal.

So you lie, waiting
Helpless; exposed.
Your visions are sketched
As you carelessly doze.

And what if the morning's
Light doesn't come?
There you'll be trapped,
By what could have been done.

Soul Food

I'll give to you my soul,
But I cannot give my heart.
For it belongs to another.
Still, I would give the moon
And the stars to you, and
Even the sky above.

Were it in my reach,
I would give your heart's desire
Upon a silver platter.
To me, your love is a sacred treasure,
Like the riches of Midas,
Or the crown jewels.
I hold your love close,
Always with me –
To brighten my darkest day.

Unforgettable

The time we spent together
So long in the past
Forever at the forefront
The images still last

I guess I should forget you
But somehow I just can't
Your cologne, it still lingers
Like a movie by Van Sant

Now and then I wonder
What you're doing now
Who you're spending time with
If you're alone somehow

Why can't I erase you, from
The annals of my mind
No one else compares
You're not like those I find

You have permeated through
Each and every pore
The less I have of you
Makes me want you more and more

www.ingramcontent.com/pod-product-compliance
Lightning Source LLC
Chambersburg PA
CBHW032142040426
42449CB00005B/359